JOSEPH'S COAT OF MANY COLORS

Contributing Writer
Marlene Targ Brill

Consultant
David M. Howard, Jr., Ph.D.

Illustrations
Gary Torrisi

Publications International, Ltd.

Long ago, in the land of Canaan, lived a man named Jacob. He had many children. Of all his children, Jacob loved his son Joseph best. To show his love, Jacob made a bright, colorful robe for Joseph.

Joseph had ten older brothers. They were jealous of Jacob's gift to Joseph.

One night, Joseph had two dreams. He told his brothers that the dreams showed that they would bow down to him someday. This made the brothers even angrier.

Soon after this, Joseph's brothers went out to take care of their father's animals. After a while Jacob told Joseph to go out and see how his brothers were doing.

When the brothers saw Joseph coming and wearing his special robe, they became angry all over again. They tore off the robe and threw Joseph into an empty pit.

Later, they saw a group of traders passing by. They decided to sell Joseph to the traders.

The brothers killed a goat and dipped the robe in the blood. Then they showed it to their father.

"It is my son's coat," Jacob cried. "A wild animal must have killed him." Jacob wept and wept.

Meanwhile, Joseph had been sold as a slave in Egypt. A man by the name of Potiphar bought Joseph and put him in charge of all he owned. Then one day, Joseph was blamed for something he didn't do. But Potiphar did not believe Joseph was innocent.

Joseph was thrown into the pharaoh's prison. He shared a cell with two men; one had been the pharaoh's baker and the other his chief cupbearer. One night, the cupbearer had a dream. Joseph explained the dream, and what he said came true. Soon, the pharaoh let the cupbearer out of jail and gave him his job back.

Joseph spent two more years in jail. But one night, the pharaoh had two dreams that upset him. The cupbearer told him about Joseph and how he had explained dreams in prison.

The pharaoh sent for Joseph. Joseph told him, "These dreams mean that there will be seven good years. Crops will grow and food will be plentiful. Then there will be seven bad years. No food will grow and the people will be hungry."

Joseph told the pharaoh to choose a wise man to collect food during the good years. This food would feed people during the bad years. The pharaoh liked this plan and put Joseph in charge.

The pharaoh told people to bow down to Joseph. Now only the pharaoh was greater in Egypt than Joseph.

Everything happened just as Joseph had said. When the bad years arrived, Joseph opened the storehouses. He sold bread to people who came from all over the world.

Back in Canaan, Jacob's family needed food, too. He sent his sons to Egypt to buy bread, but he kept his youngest son Benjamin home.

The brothers came to Joseph and bowed down. They did not recognize him, but Joseph recognized them! He pretended not to know them and asked who they were. "We are ten of twelve brothers from Canaan. The youngest is at home. One brother is no more."

Joseph had a plan. He said his brothers were spies and had them put in prison. When they were allowed to go home, Joseph said they had to return to Egypt and bring back Benjamin, the youngest brother, to prove that they were telling the truth.

The brothers returned and told Jacob what had happened. They brought Benjamin back to Egypt with them. When Joseph saw Benjamin, he was happy and sad at the same time.

Later, when the brothers were ready to leave, Joseph had sacks of grain prepared for his brothers. But he had his servants hide a silver cup inside Benjamin's sack. Then, when the brothers had left, Joseph sent guards to catch up with them. They found the silver cup and brought all of the brothers back to Joseph.

Joseph said he would let the brothers go, but that Benjamin would have to stay with him as a servant. They were so upset that Joseph could not keep his secret anymore.

"It was God, not you, who sent me here," he told them. "God made me ruler over the pharaoh's land to keep you alive."

After this, Jacob moved his whole family to Egypt. The pharaoh gave them the best land, and they lived there happily for many years.